house
made
of
rain

OTHER BOOKS BY
PAMELA PORTER

Late Moon (Ronsdale Press, 2013)

No Ordinary Place (Ronsdale Press, 2012)

I'll Be Watching (Groundwood Books, 2011)

This Awakening to Light (Leaf Press, 2010)

Cathedral (Ronsdale Press, 2010)

The Intelligence of Animals
(Backwaters Press, 2008)

Yellow Moon, Apple Moon
(Groundwood Books, 2008)

Stones Call Out (Coteau Books, 2006)

The Crazy Man (Groundwood Books, 2005)

Sky (Groundwood Books, 2004)

Poems for the Luminous World
(Frog Hollow Press, 2002)

house
made
of
rain

– poems –

PAMELA PORTER

RONSDALE

HOUSE MADE OF RAIN
Copyright © 2014 Pamela Porter

RONSDALE PRESS
3350 West 21st Avenue
Vancouver, B.C., Canada V6S 1G7
www.ronsdalepress.com

Typesetting: Julie Cochrane, in New Baskerville 11 pt on 13.5
Cover Design & Photography: Julie Cochrane
Paper: Enviro 100 Edition, 55 lb. Antique Cream (FSC) — 100%
    post-consumer waste, totally chlorine-free and acid-free

Ronsdale Press wishes to thank the following for their support of its publishing
program: the Canada Council for the Arts, the Government of Canada through
the Canada Book Fund, the British Columbia Arts Council, and the Province
of British Columbia through the Book Publishing Tax Credit Program.

Library and Archives Canada Cataloguing in Publication

Porter, Pamela, 1956–, author
    House made of rain / Pamela Porter.

Poems.
Issued in print and electronic formats.
ISBN 978-1-55380-341-6 (print)
ISBN 978-1-55380-342-3 (ebook) / ISBN 978-1-55380-343-0 (pdf)

    I. Title.

PS8581.O7573H68 2014   C811'.6   C2014-903234-X   C2014-903235-8

At Ronsdale Press we are committed to protecting the environment. To this
end we are working with Canopy (formerly Markets Initiative) and printers to
phase out our use of paper produced from ancient forests. This book is one
step towards that goal.

Printed in Canada by Marquis Book Printing, Quebec, Canada

to Rob, Cecilia, and Drew
my refuge, my strength,
and my joy

ACKNOWLEDGEMENTS

My gratitude is extended to the following magazines and books in which poems in this collection have previously appeared:

"A Story of Stone" in *FreeFall*

"Once, in a Story" in *Freefall*; winner of the *Freefall* Magazine Poetry Prize

"First World" in *Prairie Fire*

"Three Coins" in *Prairie Fire*

"Pneuma," in *Love in the Time of Predators* by Leaf Press

Additionally, I wish to express my gratitude to everyone at Ronsdale Press, especially Ronald Hatch, for their continued support of my work. I would like to thank Russell Thorburn for his sensitive ordering of the poems in this book. Thanks also go out to my fellow poets at Planet Earth Poetry, the Ocean Wilderness and Honeymoon Bay retreats, and the Waywords for their support and encouragement. Finally, I would like to thank my family — my shining lights — and Patrick and Lorna, my best teachers.

CONTENTS

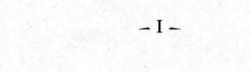

–I–

Atonement

i

And rain at the window beating its many wings.

There's a lintel over me, a threshold,
and beyond the doorframe, a furrowed dark field
on which nothing has been planted.

I keep dreaming of mountains, snow
                              stained by a low sun.
I don't know how to say goodbye,
or if I already have, or if it has been said for me.
I glorified him in my poems.

We entered a church open for prayer,
the janitor seated at the piano.
                        He can't read music
though the notes come in a rush.
The priest says it's a gift from God.

There is something in the world we call love,
that blows in of a sudden, then vanishes —
its secrets mysterious to me.

A hush fell on the morning when his music stopped,
like a river whose water has run out
leaving the mossy-haired stones
                        helpless to the flighty air.
And love, like a Holy Ghost, arrives and departs at whim.

ii

I crumble the bitter leaf, repentance, into my tea
and compose my smile, should I see him again,
and mark my escape, noting the position
                                    of every door.

How old was I when I stopped flying?
Oh, the dreams I had, the lightness in my body.
I'm all stone now.

The moon, too.
She won't get out of bed till after midnight.
                        My window's dark,
branches beat holes in the sky.
There's a bright world beyond; I see it now.

I stood on the docks as his ship carried him away
among sea ice and shards of wind;
I looked down to find the christening bottle
                        he'd placed in my hand.

The ship's horn lasts a few seconds, then silence,
but a silence with the memory of sound
                                alive in the body,
the frigid air flaming in a minor chord.

Not even the winter jasmine's frozen blossoms
                        could survive this cold.

iii

I asked the moon, and the leaves replied in a brittle voice:
                                        We covered your eyes.
Then owl-call in daylight — that curved, rung bell.
I can hear snow drifting on the other side of the mountains.

I fell under a spell — that's all there is to it.
I asked him to be my father.
Neither bone of his bone nor blood of his blood,
                        I had no right.
But cared for him as if I were his daughter.
                That was the start of it.

There is nothing and no one to blame.
                        People just do what they do,
and clouds go on scraping the mountain,
and the firs dream of birds returning.

I believed in prayer, oh, yes —
the spirits spoke to me, they did, and it was true
what they told me out of the rutted canyons
                                of their throats,
their sentences broken off in the arthritic trees.

Somewhere the world is simple. Take me there.
Here, calamity wakes early, scattering her torn scarves,
making of them the playthings of air.

Now fog has gathered the fields,
the lichen-studded trees,
and the worn and faded dead lie
                unable to raise their heads.

I remained innocent. In devotion, in betrayal.
And found myself at a great depth,
the water dark, and tasting of stone.

iv

These, my days of atonement.
I will put away my poems.
I will give up being a poet.
A ferry horn sounds; another ship departs, its migrants
                                    sipping tea in lit windows.

The horses stand inside their breath,
the pond hard, milky as bone.
I wait for the rain to make it whole again.

How to account for my life — the sins of omission,
                                    the sins of commission,
the unintended consequence of naïveté.

Sent out from heaven, I never learned to belong to earth.
Here, you're not supposed to care too much.
Love's that frightening,
                        even when you want nothing.

Beside the open doors of cathedrals I stop, hoping
the choir's anthem will tell me
                        where the shining things are hidden.
It's no wonder birds build nests in the rafters.
Someone has stitched silence into the music — the split moment
air stops shivering the grass, the doe's just flicked an ear.

How fragile we are — a word shatters us.
And me ready to make a fool of myself time after time.
Now in the mirror I look on my criminal face.
My rough nest is stuffed with loot:
                        shells, rocks, hearts, words.
I don't know how to give them back.
And that wild, prowling sun is on to me,
                           watching my every move.
Worn to their whorled spines, the shells are useful to no one,
but it's the hearts I'm most greedy for.

Everything we love was never ours to begin with.
God litters the fields with blossoms, then snatches them back.
Also the moon — here and gone. And light —
                    just try to keep some for yourself.

v

I can disappear, you know,
invisibility one of my best talents.
Every morning I walk unnoticed among the grasses,
pass unseen by alders and firs,
.   by the birds,
the crow overhead who carves himself into that blue.

I can be more still than air,
                            can fall faster than water.
As a child I perfected my art, and later
faded from pale to gossamer behind my children.

Even God, daily checking his ledger
(the print too small — his agèd eyes),
                            overlooks my name.
That's why he's neglected to come for me,
his little new moon, his shadow the clouds extinguish.
                    Call me mole, mouse, vole,
that which scurries from beneath the horses' hooves.
Droplet of mist. The echo's last repeat.

Evenings I recite my rosary of barbed wire,
and hoard my sins, those fistfuls of straw, in a corner of the barn.
Most days, they harm no one.

And like the beasts, the insomniac stars, all you'll find of me
                            are my eyes in the dark.

vi

Clearly, I have misunderstood the world.
Its yearly insistence on resurrection.
And the heart's shuttered windows keep on
        letting it in, riding on that river of blood.

Even with sky filling my mouth, I can't form the words
to undo my own desolation.

The clotted earth is thinking again, I know it,
of some invisible hand to pull it out of this long, slow death.
For months now, these branches have worn
                                only pearls of rain,
and the leafless willow drags her hair
like the Magdalene at Christ's feet —
                that outrageous gesture.

I spread my fingers and the piano tells my story.
Once upon a time, it begins, and ends badly,
the final, broken chord singing,
                you remain fatherless, dear.

And me with no compass.
The trees point in all directions. And the stars —
meek smiles that mask a cold indifference.

But some nights I dream of palaces —
                the soul's memory of heaven
where the miraculous — wild, green-eyed —
prowls the halls on its four mute paws.

vii

Mark this place,
that all who pass by will know
                              an accident has occurred.
Plant crosses; clutch in your fist
the spent lives of brittle blossoms. Say,
                              grief visited us,
say, a door has blown open, the wind escaped
with his plunder.

There was a crescent-bowed bridge.
There was water, and his face, turned to me
                              turned stern, stone.
I give back every word I have taken.
The wild and the tame. Those that sleep.
Those with terror on their faces.
The forsaken piled like refuse in the kitchen sink.
My fingerprints are all over them.

Strung into chains, locked onto my ankles,
thus we could shuffle to the drowning pond,
or, fed to the lantern, they'd blaze the path
                              to disgrace.

In the field, dark-eyed horses.
One rings the gate with a hoof.
And the land falls away into distance,
toward mist risen from the last rain
as though, walking through,
                              you'd step into another world.

What was it I wanted from him all this time?
                    Tea, and conversation.
Lace of the Japanese maple blazing in the sun.

viii

Remember: when the angels cried their coyote cries
                                   as the sun went down.
I have asked them to return, make a ceremony of this sundering.
Already the jasmine hangs her yellow flowers in shame.
                         Someone's told her it's sinful,
that blooming — so extravagant and out of season.

I commit my unrighteous heart to solitary.
Clang the door closed. Pocket the keys.
Grant me a quiet extinction: to become the air,
water that stumbles shallow over stone,
        a dried husk fluted by the breeze.
I'm small enough, and getting smaller,
can blend into the dark, take up no space at all.

And I confess, I confessed to all his accusations
                    both true and untrue.
Useless it was to argue.

Then he was done with me, bundled me up,
launched me downstream
              in my basket of reeds.
Dusted the river silt from his palms.

Derelict, adrift among cattails and the chatter of flitting birds,
those first days I sent out notes in bottles:
                    I'm all right. Don't worry about me.

Time might put it differently.
How simple an act to throw someone away.
How, counting out the hours, I shook out seeds;
how everything sewn refused life,
                         but light.
Such abandon — growing by the hour, the day,
thriving as it did, on neglect.

ix

The taste of loss in my mouth.
The smell of loss on my hands
                    like metal, like blood.
There was no snow. But you could say
the snow buried everything,
and you'd be right. You could say
he saw a boulder,
                    she saw an animal.
You could stand at the end of the tree-lined path
and see one view at morning,
                                    another at evening.
There may by a reasonable explanation,
                    or there may not.
You could say the rains came
                    and buried the snow,
that the snow lay down, too tired to be snow anymore.
The broad, brown leaves of the maple
that once fell from a height,
felt the air hold, then let go,
then lay themselves tight against earth —
you could say the snow sank
into their flat leaf faces,
                    their spread, webbed fingers,
that the snow leaned into them as if into another body —
there is sadness, longing, emptiness in the act.

All this can occur inside a person.
In the wide and barren landscape, the expanse we carry.
But now in the landscape there is no longer a house,
no longer a barn, or horses.
Only the wind blown cold into our faces,
the stink of loss in the nostrils,
and in the air, coming thicker, heavier now,
snow.

x

Reliquary: bleached deer bone, washed up on shore.
A stone he handed to me still in its wet translucence.
Carapace of ocean creature, lichen attached.
                    Feathers, jagged eggshells robin-blue,
snip of horse's mane, poems that say, *Father.*
He made clear I have no father.
Poems that say, *Father,* put away for bearing false witness.

How Time slows the days just for me,
that I may consider these things over and over.

Absence: as in an empty room. A window without curtains.
A clothesline wearing only wooden pins.
Sun's hidden fist; overhead, unaltered grey.

Oh Lord, I am not worthy.
Suffer the banished to come unto me.
Suffer my hands to cover my face.
                    Suffer my ears; suffer my eyes.

Come unto me, oh dog barking in the night.
Come unto me, owl in the branched arteries of air.

Come charred moon who has blackened her face,
come angels of ash, of thorn, rust, of shattered glass.

Come thou wrenched, thou unforgiven.
                    Dust off my wings, I'm one of you.
We'll make a home among the ruin.

xi

Now the chickadees come to my window
                        to tell me of the day —
what the creek said, the gossip among the ferns
and where the cats last were seen.
I offer myself to the morning
                        and her reckless love.
The difference between us — the morning never blames herself.

When I go walking, I want my shoes
                            to leave no mark.
Nothing to say I was here, breathed this light,
was an impediment to another's happiness.
And when the sky sows its seeds of rain,
what can be the harvest but grief?

I will ask for an offering
to place at the far corner of this field,
that the days and nights allow me to live
                        unnoticed by the world,
to relinquish my life like holy water collected in mason jars,
poured out like longing, my baptism
into that which cannot be undone.

A spoon proved my final failing;
let the birds return it to him which was never mine,
                            neither his father-love.
And knowing that the tilted world, insensitive
to my feelings, will send anyway
an orchestra of bees to the heather, the odour
                            of apple blossom,
I must prepare myself
as when a piece of music, lost four hundred years,
                        is played at last —
soon as the bow is set to the strings, you know
the first note will break your heart.

xii

There's no road back, and I don't want to go there anyway.
Even the cedars look forsaken, as if to say,
is there no way out of winter,
                        all this death lying around?

From the beginning of my life on earth,
my soul twirled about in flowy dresses,
tugged at me until I followed.
                Her plan — to find him. Father.
What did she think would happen then?

All those years and so little progress.
Still she kept packing us up, moving us on.
How she found him in the end is anyone's guess.

It is terrible to live in two worlds at once,
haunted by dreams, mysterious meetings,
the heavenly membrane ripped clean away.
        Your life is not your own.
And I know how the mortal world considers
                        those who live this way.
For her audacity, he nailed me with his eyes.

Together my soul and I devoted ourselves to him.
Cookies, pies. Poems on hand-made paper.
Now she goes around under a shroud
                        she dragged out of the barn.
And me with the day's muddied chores to deal with.
That, and her unremitting grief.

xiii

Here, everything is the same as before, still the same.
                                        Daylight and darkness.
Horses huddled out of the rain.

A teacher comes Fridays to watch me ride.
The piano listens to my hands and plays
just what I tell it. No covering for mistakes.
Here, I dream of the quiet, care little for success.

The cat rides my shoulders across the field,
and when I sing, the horses swivel an ear.
Now and then the twin bucks come down,
shed of their antlers and budding new,
            like youngsters all over again.
I've always been unknown, and I don't mind;
the things he said I'd done
            were true, some of them.

Everything as before is the same
                    though he never arrives for tea.
I don't need to go anywhere, and friends don't come over.
Some nights the owl calls from far away,
but it's my little candle in the window
                    tells the darkness I'm home.

xiv

My body remembers every note of the *Pathetique*.
I'm playing it again, wonder how much
                              is imprinted on us —
the years a city in ruins to be sifted through,
its only citizen with no sense for order,
                              still, with any luck
might uncover something whole, forgotten, beautiful.

He loved me, I know it. Already
the bare willows' narrow flames
                              shoot into the sky,
the maples tensed in concentration.
I'm afraid spring will leave me behind,
              my little soul gone to bed with fever.

He loved me, he said so, treated me like a daughter
at times, and once said, "Eat your vegetables."
                    I'd scrabbled so long on my own,
it filled me with happiness.

I'm learning to live simply, to live without.
And that voice in me that chooses against despair to sing
is raising her crystal tone toward the high cedars
though I try my best to hush her, threaten her
                              with menacing glances.

No longer do I envy others their good fortune,
their fathers, their invitations.
A person can stand at a door, be let in, and in,
and suddenly, sent away. I feel it night and day, in my chest,
my own bloodied muscle, *knock, knock*
                              on unmoving bone.

Memory lives inside me, each year a country
with its borders, rivers.
Of some, all I remember of a year — the babies' fevers
              or scent of lilac, too brief,
or summer fires fed by wind
                  when we hosed down the roof.

If what I can recall is what counts for my life,
I've hardly lived. I'm barely alive.

But once, driving alone up the mountain, in headlights
a bobcat and her tuft-eared kits —
               all those lit eyes.
And for years after, expected miracles like that.

As a deer, I'd appear and disappear at will;
as a heron, I'd fold myself behind the bracken,
beseeching the gods of absolution
              while the moon grew fat on clouds
and the choirs of silence hung their lanterns over me.

             It's true, once I was ambitious,
longed to stand before a crowd.
But an unseen hand has cured me,
has brought instead this close of cedar and fern,
              and the ten-thousand-year-old rain.

xvi

        I told him, "You are the one
I looked for everywhere, the one since childhood
I searched and grieved
               as for a beloved father."
But anger rose in his face, his eyes turned to ice.

I should learn to stop blurting out the truth.

           And now each evening
I ask forgiveness of the shrouded sky, the moon gone gaunt.
But my soul's not holding her breath.
When I'm busy feeding horses,
raising the manure fork to the wheelbarrow,
                  she's digging a hole.
I've watched her climb in, test
to see how much deeper she has to dig,
thinks she can choose to be mortal.

Even this early I've seen a robin,
and soon the field will be filled with them
sticking their noses in the dirt. Already
           the plum trees' tight buds.

Maybe she'll give up on this rock-laden soil
           and build a tomb instead.
Whatever ending she wanted wasn't this,
the road we travelled so long to find him
           blocked now by a great stone.

xvii

Our time on earth is fleeting, she read
in the big book,
                    the blink of an eye, an instant.
Barefoot, in a hair shirt, she's out carrying a candle
among the clustered oaks, their dendrite branches,
the snow moon timid behind the pines.

With the dark eyes of an animal, she looks to me
                              and I know her question.
And answer, *We were charged with deceit.*
Truth is, he didn't want a daughter.
Truth was, he didn't want me for a daughter.
Who can blame him? It's easier not to love
                              if you don't have to.

Now my diminutive soul wants to know
                              why he left us,
and I say, *I am guilty, guilty; I refused
          to lock up my imprudent heart,*
while we stand looking up a slender tree,
branches bowed as cathedral staves,
and wait for holy water to land on our tongues
                              to bless us, to guarantee
our hearts will be broken and broken,
as we hurtle among the fisted stars
and stumble on unhealed.

xviii

Now that I am stripped to ground,
                         make me over again.
Make my life a simple song —
the fractured flight a winged seed makes
at the pleasure of the wind.
                         Ruah. Ruah. Lauda.
Make me simple again.

You, thing unnamable, your heaven-shadow lurking
                         over my sleep,
You more intimate than breath
who are nightmare and storm, and snow's silent birth,
             who are each grain of night.
You enter me and seize my heart.
Again. Again. Again.

Tear out my fear. Steal my sorrow, take my need.
Whisper in the most silent forests of my self,
             in music's pure voice, as you sang
in the moment of my first stung note.
As the wolf moon scavenges the hills,
and water drips dark in the laced caverns of earth,
as the million million mouths of stars
have forever sung your song.

             Make me simple.
Teach me to sing with my imprisoned tongue.

    Louez. Kyrie. Alabaré.

Make my life your song.

xix

Each day I go on doing what I do,
while the two bucks feed by the creek,
          the three does graze the field,
as the horses chase each other
or sleep with a hind hoof cocked, fearing no predator,
the wind in the branches
          blowing tears onto my face.

Animals make good company, as does light,
though the moon, impetuous sister,
          has sunk again into her shell,
skulking behind that flat grey stone.
And a flock of black birds at dusk
                    rises as one,
like ash blown free from the night's burnt stars.

Every night holds an ancient hour
where anything can happen,
          any dream can occur.

I go on living in a forest filled with firs
who stand unmoving
                    like silent, impervious fathers.
I could choose any of them,
but not one, even in a storm, calls me by name.

XX

Once there lived a young couple who were very poor and wished to find a small spot on which to build a cottage and make a life together. The two set out from their village and followed a deer trail up the mountain, looking for a place which they could call home. Already the woman was with child and was obliged to stop and rest many times along the route. After hours climbing high above the village, they chose a narrow plot of land near an alpine meadow, whereupon the young man took out a pickaxe and began to carve out of the mountain their home.

With time, and much effort on the young man's part, he managed a dwelling with two rooms and a door which sat between two square windows. Then he set about making a bed, a table, a cradle for the infant and, as an afterthought, dug out a small loft where the child would sleep in a few years' time. Unfortunately, it happened that one winter's day on an excursion into the village, the young man was caught up in an avalanche and perished, leaving his wife alone to give birth to a baby girl.

In the years that followed, the child thrived under her mother's care. Before a dozen years had passed, however, her mother grew ill and weak, and the child learned to cook and clean, and care for her mother through the many long months until she died. The girl then lived by herself on the mountainside, making her living by sewing items to sell in the village, as her mother had done, and taught the girl to do. By day she stitched and gathered firewood and berries, and by night she asked the stars to bring her a father, a prayer she had made each night before sleep from the time she was very young. But she continued with the prayer more fervently now that her mother, too, was gone.

One day as she was gathering berries and fuel for a fire, a man with silvering hair neared the cottage, followed at his heels by his companion, a wolf. The girl, greeting him, believed the stars had answered her prayer at last. Questioning how a girl of twelve could survive on a mountainside alone, the man was shown the cottage tucked so tightly into the face of the mountain, only the door was immediately visible; but on closer inspection, he noticed two small windows of uneven glass, one on either side of the door. The girl took note of his pleasant countenance and gentle eyes, and said to him, "You, sir, are the father I have beseeched of the stars, night after night, for as long as I can remember."

Eventually the man and his wolf settled in to the small room that had first belonged to the young couple, and then to the girl's mother, while the girl continued to sleep in the loft on her straw pallet under the low ceiling of exposed stone. Their days together flowed easily one into the other, and their fondness for each other blossomed.

Mornings, the girl wakened to a fire crackling in the hearth, but would lie still until her father called to her, and then they would venture outdoors to check the traps which he had taught her to set for hares and ground squirrels. Evenings, they ate the meat which they cooked over the fire, along with the girl's biscuits and berries, the wolf curled in a corner away from the heat of the hearth, and later, they'd lie on their backs in the summer grass as he pointed out the stars, their vast array, and he told her how she could find her way by following certain stars.

One morning the father gave the girl a test, and commanded her to sew him a quilt, to be made not of cloth but of leaves, and lined with moss. "If you love me, you will finish the quilt by sunrise tomorrow," he said, believing the task he had given her to be impossible for a girl to complete. The girl thought his command curious, but since she had prayed so many years for his coming, she knew she loved him very much indeed, and had also grown fond of the wolf.

The girl spent the day gathering leaves which had begun to fall from the trees in rich colours of yellow and red. She gathered these into her basket, as well as moss which she rolled and carried under one arm. In her loft, the girl began to piece the quilt into a repeating pattern of colour. As she did so, she became more and more excited for the gift she would present to her father, for whom she felt deep gratitude. Under his care and attention, the girl felt stronger than she had ever felt, as though she could do anything, and would give him a quilt more beautiful than he had ever imagined a quilt could be.

The girl sewed each leaf with her most careful, her finest stitching. She worked all night and did not, even for a moment, close her eyes to rest. As dawn approached and the early light began to brighten the windows and then the floor of the cottage, she completed her final stitches.

Her father, just risen and dressed, had stepped outside to gather firewood. With the quilt folded over one arm, the red and gold leaf pattern flowing like a waterfall from her arm to the floor, the girl hurried down the ladder from her loft, and ran out the door to show him the exquisite creation she had made.

"Look, Father, your quilt is finished, just as you commanded!" Upon which, the father, his silvered hair shining in the morning sun, studied the quilt. He took it from her outstretched hands, felt the softness of the moss stitched between the layers of the quilt, examined the pattern of light to dark which the leaves made.

Suddenly his eyes darkened with anger. "You love me too much!" he exclaimed, his face reddening with rage, the quilt tossed from his hands to lie crumpled on the ground.
As the girl stared up at her beloved father, she felt a wind stir, which lifted her hair, her skirt. The wind grew stronger, fiercer, as she watched her father's face turn from red to brown, then brittle as winter-dried leaves. Then, to the girl's astonishment, his shoulders, his arms and hands, then all of him turned to brown, brittle leaves which the wind thrust high into the air, toward the tops of the trees, the peak of the mountain.

Now no one stood before the girl; only the rumpled quilt lay on the damp ground. From the corner of her eye, she glimpsed the wolf disappearing into the trees. For many nights afterward, as she lay in her loft waiting for sleep, she could hear the wolf howling its high-pitched notes, each night from a greater distance, the sound coming fainter and fainter, until at last the night came when she could hear no cry at all.

xxi

I wake and she is standing beside the bed,
my soul, bewildered, no taller than a child,
little boat moored in this earthen hour.
                    How stupid of me
to think he'd be my father, I tell her;
now we must open our hands,
                    release him, knowing
he will choose other daughters.

See, on the path, dead,
                    a bird, its song flown.
See, half hidden behind the barn
                    this famine moon.

She climbs into bed beside me
and soon is sleeping, neither anxious nor sad,
neither fugitive nor joyful. I try to touch her small hands,
                              her dress, her cheek,
but touch nothing; her body in stillness moves
as waves of light flicker across a mirror, a white page.

How night passes into day, and again into night
                              so quietly you can hear it,
as the earth clasps her deep green secrets to her chest.

xxii

He has gone silent as the dead are silent,
                 as *Our Father which art in heaven.*
But perhaps it is we who are the dead,
who listen in our underground offices
to the night's voice spreading its brackish water,
the moon, bright wafer,
                        broken in two.

My soul has laid a cedar frond on her arm,
strokes it with a finger as though she were a god,
her world this chain of green mountains, sea-fed inlets
pale as a drifted field beneath words on a page.

Who was that woman who bore my name,
my history, the colour of my hair,
of whom it was said heard voices,
to whom poetry came in abundance
                  like bushels of ripe pears —
did she turn down another road in the dark,
lost among the unlit streets of a besieged city?

As for me, the program has been carried out:
I have received my sentence,
                  and without the bother of a trial.
Having saved up my transgressions,
he laid them down like branches the day
I entered Jerusalem on my narrow hooves.

If I have appeared in anyone's dream, I apologize.
                     It won't happen again.
One day, the gatekeepers will show me
which were my sins, and which were not.
For now, I have folded up,
                  a leaf of no use to the tree,
fallen from a height, limp from months of rain.

xxiii

I have forgotten my name.
Nights I dream all the names for river, for loss,
the signatures of grass,
                              dead letters carved into stone.
But when I awake I remember no one's name,
                              not even my own.

Names for birth, for drought,
                              for those who have given up,
all the colours of snow and shadow.
My little soul says her name is Fortune.
But the dozen letters of my name have risen
as rain hurled from the wind-bent firs,
                              have buried themselves,
little black seeds in the ploughed rows of soil.

                    And I will remain nameless
as the dusted eyelids of moths, as the rose's skin,
the jasmine's fallen yellow.

                    When my children call to me now,
their voices will be the sound of water
                              tumbling down the air,
the sound a paw makes breaking the surface
of a pond.

My name will be the clamour of blood
turning back from the tips of my fingers,
                    and my forsaken heart
scratching stories into the bone-cave of my chest.

I am a songbird without song,
a trout swimming against Time's river.
Even now I am nameless night, who waits, sleepless
for light's cloven hoof to leave her track
                              in the red mud of dawn.

xxiv

She has become a bird today.
              Exhausted by this human road,
she has turned to bird, and flits among the pregnant branches,
her tongue a dark flame
                     narrow as light beneath a door.

Dawn envies the blush of her chest,
             dusk, all the colours of her song.
Wind wants to wrap her like a scarf,
make music over the hollow of her bones.

I have been in the house throwing things out,
making room for the rest of my life,
whispering, *I did not deceive him.*
             I did not deceive him.

But she sings from the cathedral roof of her beak
                to the wide arc of morning,
and the mosses raise all their ears to her song.

XXV

Overnight, infant leaves were born.
Overnight, Moon gathered up her skirt,
slid past the stars and over the edge of the world.

Overnight, I lost a father.
Last year's leaves crowded the shore
                              and nearly became stone.

This grief is an ancient town
buried a thousand years, only now awakened.

This grief is one comma on a page of a book so weighty
            you have to hold it in both your arms.

This grief is one snowflake in a night gone white with their falling,
                                          hour upon hour,
and goes on falling even after we've risen from bed
        to stand at the window, spellbound, all morning.

Overnight, Moon slid past the stars
            and disappeared, like a father.
Overnight, infant leaves were born. This morning
their green faces shine, wet with ancient tears.

xxvi

If my tongue does not forget my mouth,
if my hands do not forget my face
                    nor my fingers their song;
if my ears do not forget the words
            they fold into my brain,
if my brain does not forget the dream
in its stone well of sleep,
                        in its ocean
filled with schools of dreams darting
                    through sunlit water;
if my feet do not forget distance, or proximity,
if my eyes do not refuse the truth
or my mouth neglect to speak it,
and if, in my sleep I fly to the country
                    where poetry is born,
if I find my way further on toward nurseries of light,
the nebulae where love is formed
                from stars and dust,
if I become a church, if I turn into music,
if in my sleep I begin to hear inside the morning
newborn birds noisy in the newborn air,
if the roof over my bed becomes the sky,
if, even though awakened, I still could fly,
                    if my heart becomes the sun
and my blood stains the wan edge of earth,
if an invisible hand, if unseen fingers
stitch my heart whole again,
if the child living inside me remains a child
and forgiveness folds its wings at the windowsill
                            and makes a home,
        if a voice clear as cathedral bells,
if a voice like bells speaks, if it commands
                    Take up thy bed and walk,
if I hear, if I do, if it is the answer
to pain, to sorrow, to unknowing, to everything.

xxvii

A riddle: *A stone that is mortal as we are mortal.*
Answer: The moon — it is born, waxes, wanes, and dies.

Another riddle, not so simple this time:
                              the night's one eye a lamp:
the lamp lights the passage to a place
the eye knows so well, even while falling asleep
the eye can find the spot
                    without compass —
a mountain, through which rivers flow underground,
their ebb and flow ruled by a queen
      in a palace whose walls, like the mountain,
 are more rigid than iron, more crumbling than bone.

And in her queendom two flowers drink
from that dark water: one, a rose
with a stem of thorns; the other, a peony
                          carved into stone.
If you ask each flower its name, both will answer:
      Remembrance.

            But what are these flowers?
Certainly, each is more than its name.
Answer: the rose, forgiveness; the peony, death.

And the mountain? What is the mountain
                  whose rivers flow underground?
Answer: the heart.

But death has visited us even now:
windows boarded up, doors locked
                        and no one remaining inside the house,
the house a kind of body with a heart inside.
But the heart has left the body
                  as a bird escapes a paw,
the feathered, delicate, dark-eyed music
that is the heart, singing,
flying on its scalloped passage,
              that clear breath, *Ruah,*
without which the world would fall to ruin.

There is only so much time. And even now
              a death has carved itself into this day,
here, just over the border from eternity,
where things constantly go wrong.

And the moon fallen asleep.
And the porch lamp flickering, bullied by wind.
Soon, rain will begin.

xxviii

Lately, I've been making excuses
so as to decline invitations. I'm sick,
I say, or, the car is broken,
                one of the horses gone lame.

        How can I speak the truth —
that I must grieve this season.
Which is not self-explanatory
                and requires discussion:
I asked him to be my father.
I loved him, but did not please him.

That's why the bells have gone silent,
                        and also the cellos.
That's why the deer, when they see me,
shift their hooves awkwardly beside the water;
soon the trees and then the hills
                start acting embarrassed,
and that's the moment I go inside.

But a few afternoons when I stood crying
                at the edge of the field,
the grey tabby with white paws
                        climbed the fencepost
and settled on my shoulders.

Animals will put a thought in your head.
She said, everything moves in seasons.
She said, we spend only part of our lives here.

Daily she praises the wildness between her paws
and the bowls that leaves become
                when filled and overflowing with rain.

xxix

My little soul gathers them into the vessels of her hands,
                    these fragments of dawn,
this fragrant snow tinted with the long low sun.

She has hundreds of names for them:
                    little feathers of winged trees,
flown ash from the birthplace of suns.
Artifacts of an ancient horizon.
                    Kissed eyelids, moths,
the night's numberless secrets,
the plum trees' cold tissue of breath.
Little messengers that whisper, *release, release.*

Still the blushed blossoms break apart,
ravished by wind, fallen into mud and water,
                                    onto stone,
tangled in the horses' manes.

These petals that have never stopped falling
onto the emperors' *koi* ponds,
on the rough-hewn steps
                    of the haiku master's house,
onto samovars and tea spoons and linen
beside the Black Sea.

When darkness comes,
the blossoms, as they always have done,
become the sacred scripture of rain,
the smallest of owls,
                    the moon.

What will we remember of our time here
where shadows blossomed into grief,
where we couldn't know just by looking
which stars were alive
                and which died centuries ago;

how we'd recite the heart's litanies
                          of despair and wonder
if this life were an elaborate dream,
our delicate houses vanished at our waking.

We'll speak of the way we held
        forgiveness in our pockets,
reached in and felt it there,
forgiveness ready any moment
        to be given and given away.

We'll say, how hard we tried.
How hard we tried to love.

– II –

Call Her Name

Tonight the owl in the pine cries out and hears
only its own cry in the air, curved like the earth
and the oncoming dark. And light
bequeaths to the night its many countries
on both sides of my window: in one, a lamp
and a book; in another, the late-blooming rose,
  an owl, a bitten moon.
        In those days
the child climbed the sycamore into the dizzying air
where no one thought to find her. Standing in the sky
she could see the man leave by the front door and walk
down the street to his car, could hear her mother
     close the door behind him.
And the child told no one what she knew,
her tongue a broken clapper inside a bell.

What does a river know that an ocean does not?
Something about time's secret life overfilling its banks.
And the owl hidden in the trees
     is God calling God,
while darkness spills itself over the flowers.

In her mind the child believed at any moment
her father might turn the corner of her street.
  Knowing neither his name nor his face,
she wondered if he would come walking or by car.

Sometimes on a dirt road that measures one horizon to another,
I've seen a silent animal emerge from the wheat
just after the sun's death,
the eyes alone on the road and staring.
                            Alone with time,
the child waited in the sycamore, heat ironing her skin
until the windows lit the yard, until her mother
                  called and called her name,
and hearing no sound, turned back inside.
Then the child climbed down.

There was snow that year we buried the mare;
barbed wire hobbled the fence posts, the earth
turning around its new wound, snow
                  that lit the night, the pines
laying their thin shadows down. I slept and woke
as the sorrel whinnied on and on, the moon
searching the sea for what had drowned.

Inside the house was a smashed cup and her mother
kneeling on the kitchen floor. And the girl knew
        there were laws of arrival and departure.
From her bed she considered climbing the night's branches
and saw herself in them, looking down
                      from the glittering leaves.

When I returned to the place in Spring, the prayers
I had strung across the brook were gone.
                              And tonight the owl
crying out and flying, the rose high on the trellis
opening her white face.
                  And then they left that house
and drove to a place of trees without number.
The girl chose the largest oak,
which wore on its branches a dress of lace.
First she nailed boards up the trunk and understood
she must be ever vigilant
with her father not knowing where to find her.

And the oak just outside her window.
She wondered if the branch that nearly touched her
would hold her weight. And how her mother
wanted the tree felled.

The moon grown round, perched in the night,
                        its ears hidden under down.

The Dead Do not Dream of Me

My dead have grown numerous
                    as shore birds,
as the sparks from dry boards
when the old wheat bin
                    burned after rain.
One held lilacs to her face. One
                    flew from a bridge,
her wet skirt wrapping her legs.
Another lit cigarettes in the dark.
On the street, you could hear
The Pearl Fishers
                    booming from the house.
I go into the lingering daylight,
the moon sliding down,
but hear no music from the dead.

I flew back through the open door
           from which I came, all bitten
wing and wind, and vanished
through the hole of my mouth. Child,
I am finished with this earth.

— — —

In the window it is winter.
           Even the dog now gone.
Branches hold nothing but lichen and sky
and remnants of the rain.
Crows mark the fog.
I cannot go into death
           in search of them.

Even your name is not your name.
Even our death is not our death.
We are a house inside a house;
you are the hours not yet born.

— — —

Mother was prettiest after the war.
She rode seated backward on a train.
The light on the river, the wheat
                    still green.
She saw nothing of what was to come.
On her lap, two pears, one plum.

I wonder now if I imagined that year —
snow on the mimosa,
                    or the sandstorm
rolling over us, blotting out the sun.
Someone calling and calling my name.
And now I'm the only one
                    who's lived to tell it.
I've heard the stones speak, and flocks of geese
when they rise from the pond.
I have dreamed a road composed of light.
But the dead do not dream of me.

I dream still of opening myself, ravished,
                    in shadowed rooms
and have swept up all their names
and filled my pockets with their dust.
I keep my secrets, child, crumpled in my fists
so that you never know
from whom you were made.

— — —

And what name do I answer to?
Somewhere a box of letters.
In June, the sun refuses to go down,
the horses in high grass swishing their tails.
        The dead snagged on the world,
their lives folded up, a piece of cloth, a leaf.
The dead do not write to me.

Gray limbs against the sky, we scratch
out our names, as though we never were.

— — —

We have this treasure in earthen vessels,
writes Paul, *death works in us.*
I carry the taste of blood on my lip,
and the moon, light from my candle
     sending back messages in code.
Sometimes the trees wave wildly to the stars,
but the dead do not pass through the veil to me.

What remnant we are we have placed
in you — wet stone, a lump of ice, ring
of soot. It was I who broke the vase,
and I who tore the cloth
     trembling on the line.
We are the dead; we are finished
with this earth.

— — —

Last night, the owls. Crying, not
as usual across the distant dark,
but soft, having found each other at last.
I stand to grieve or to praise,
                    open a book
and read aloud by lamplight
words of invocation, of intercession.
I have searched through absence,
broken narrative,
                    photographs.
Let the dead come to me.

Let grief be enough. Leave us
in the dark, beneath the coal-smoked
earth. Begin again
          to name each thing:
say water, say breath.
          Say empty. Say heart.

Pneuma

In the morning I could find no sign of her
imprinted near the water.

As I slept in a house beside a river,
                                    a cougar came.
And beneath my window, screamed.

Some part of her walked through me
then continued down the hall
toward my children
                    asleep in their cribs.
Sinew, shoulders, spine, she parted the night.

And claimed us. And required of us
        suffering, and bereavement, and joy.
And sentenced us to live
in immensity's open mouth.

It is the oldest story.
Something searches for us,
            and when it finds our lives,
returns over and over.

I never know when she will arrive
or take her leave.
        But like the echo of a prior bell,
she circles inside me,
                cold, delicate,
her four paws clotted with darkness.

Before the Day Is Over

Mother has returned
to the kitchen and is making dinner.
Pots and lids bang together on the shelf.
The spoon drawer opens and closes on its own.
                     Mother has returned,
the service not to her liking,
            though I wore the plain dress
            of mourning, and blackbirds
cried out, beating and beating the air,
and the trees' fallen fruit bloodied the walk.
Now Mother's worn thin and furious
like the time the globe of swirling snow shattered
and winter spilled over us, hoarding our love.

In the hallway the ghosts gather beside
their photographs as they have done
since my childhood, their light flaring
at the sound of Mother with her spoons.
And I hear too, wind at the corner of the house
flee like a startled horse,
              frightening the leaves, the sky
building up its resentment, and I know
where this is going; before the day is over
we'll all be left with tears on our faces.

Once, unseen behind a door, I heard her say,
           Tell him I'm dead.
And now she is, and there is no place for her
on the earth. Place there is none.

Here as in childhood, between the hours
of daughter and mother,
                    breath and ash,
candles lean from their pulpits,
each single wing attempting flight.
Light between trees fallen to the ground. The day spent.
The storm-lit sky turns to rose,
                    a wake of blossoms over us.

The Name I Carried

          Finally, I arrived
at the vanishing point of light.
How quickly the moon waned.
I had hoped for some ecstatic utterance
or any word at all,
          however ordinary.
I tore at the frayed hem of my story, all
my garments worn through,
instruments of the wind.

And no one, friend or neighbour,
to wonder what I might be doing there,
waiting inside a house no more a house,
and my dead,
          like birds, flown
forward into night, and unlike birds,
flown backward into memory.

But in a certain part of the field,
Queen Anne's lace shone,
          the grass, burnished, gleamed,
and God continued to pursue me
though I never saw him,
          and I remain fatherless.

Having lived to tell it, I wait
        for a word from the dead,
for my mother's letters to arrive
at the window: petal, wing,
                a thin line of moon.
I count over and over
the colours from burial to tears.
I am a mourning dove in the pines,
the shade of rain and ash,
        a face dreaming a face,
a candle whose flame becomes two
                        in the glass.

Now when the air fills with leaves
I know they're the children
                their father can't feed.
They cover the earth with their want.
The slip of paper in my pocket reads: *bereft.*
I've lost the name I carried
                before my birth.

The Angel of Death

She sweeps up the minutes as they pass,
this angel, the angel of death,
and carries in one basket the hours,
in another,
       the still-glimmering years,
bearing them away into the night.

Cry out for her, and she turns her back,
her skirts flaring,
       sewn from torn garments,
grief, crumpled letters, teeth,
feathers fallen from the sky.

In her hands she traps the breath, a mouse
caught beneath a cat's claws.
       Her long, desolate fingers
pull petals, one by one,
           from the rose,
and with her breath scatters them,
turning the world to scarcity
             and need.

I have seen her
       dismantle the morning,
chase the Spring into disarray.
If both the mountain and the grass
       lie down under snow,
there is no hope for the child
she lures onto the delicate,
          the terrible ice.

See the names
written on the inside of her wrist.
The way she erases the moon
        over and over.
How her voice, quiet as the sound
of oars in water,
        silences the heart.

A Story of Stone

On the shore, a stone lay waiting —
wingless golden bird,
                    burrowing tortoise,
repository of every song
            the sea has ever sung;
                        lay beyond
the receding tide, curled
inside the noisy complaint of the wind.
                    Earth's jewel,
remnant of a temple in ruin
                an ocean distant; a poem
in a language lost to time —

my father picked it up, turned it over and over,
                then laid it on my palm.

My father, who cannot live
long enough to satisfy me,
                gave to me a stone
of incomparable light and colour.

And who is to say the stone did not
                        choose him
for the many mansions of his heart,
having seen how the wind,
greedy for my father's voice,
                stole also the leftover
                    tatters of his breath.

Scratched on the hidden scrolls
of my veins are written
        verses of my gospel:
and this shall be a sign unto you —
a stone, an offering
marbled, heart-shaped, carrying its own
chambers of light and shadow,
and you shall be a witness —

to him who walks the earth
with lighter and lighter steps,
who this day scoured the shore
                        as a bird does,
knowing the worth of a thing.

And made a gift of a stone.

Once, in a Story

My mother died in a far city.
Now she lives with me, fearful
                          of her life,
stranded in the branches of afternoon.
She drinks the soup of poverty
            and slips behind the door,
hoping God won't find her there.

I found my father in a dream.
He was rowing a boat across the night,
                    searching for me
while the moon
          fell asleep behind the clouds.
And when I awoke, I discovered
the seed of him inside me,
which, fallen to die,
                    was born a book.
And all that was written in the book
came to pass.

I stood up, looked out the window,
                  and saw a road,
the one I had travelled from birth.
And the road said, *you were never alone.*

*Be careful what you say about me
        and to whom,* said the road,
and now I write poems
        I can't show to anyone.
I've walked through a doorway
                  and can't go back.

Now the meadowlark
alights on the bowing stalk and whistles,
         set the table for a guest.
The owl sits on a branch and calls,
              whose song are you?

And the moon chants, *light and dark,*
                      dark and light.

Once in a story that was called a miracle,
a man rubbed mud and spittle
         from his eyes, and saw
trees walking, a crowd of trees,
his wife and children among them.
                   And the trees
reached out their branches
and touched him with their thick leaves,
a forest murmuring above him,
         the magnificent sea overhead.

And there were more astonishments:
the hives of houses glittering in the sun,
         the road a rolled-out cloth
stitched to the hills, and darkness growing
              at the far end of light.

And there was light and there was darkness
              in the days that passed,
but no one who was present that day
                   was ever the same.

Witness

It was the searching exhausted me.
Despair, disguised as winter,
        ate and slept with me.
I did not expect to survive.

And suffered dreams, voices
of those I loved from before, the gates
shut behind us,
            and how we awoke,
strangers on earth, separated, bereft.

Each morning I watched the fires of dawn
consume the darkness, and each night
was witness
            to the sun's falling
into the great furnace burning
beneath the world.

In rain, grief streamed from me.
Forest stars at my feet,
        desert grasses flickering
            in the blue air.

And everyone having taken on new faces.
        I tell you, it was miraculous —
    a hand on my arm,
                something in their eyes,
a face glistening in the way light
returns, that unearthly brilliance
                        after a storm.

We wanted to be born.
Such wonders we could not
have imagined in the other world:
                crying, sacrifices made
        simply for love, and the day
I saw you standing far off
        in a field of wild flowers.

First World

We were born into birds, into bone, into wings,
                    mist drifting among the pines.
And gathered to ourselves plenty for this life:
loneliness to rival the sky,
perfection in the art of losing.

I had my own darkness, my face a new moon,
and planned my journey by the constellations,
                    marked them in ink on my palm.
And carried with me an empty basket, and went on
each day being born
                    into a second world and a third,
a bright music calling my name beyond all waters.

I knew my ancestry:
                    a tree fallen onto a house,
horses foraging the hopeless grass,
a map torn along its folds.
A violin missing from the case.

Not everything is held in the hands of the living.
There are winters I've only dreamed about.
                    Who would find us in our wilderness,
singing a song poured out of the wind's sleep?

I opened the book of lost words, and by lamplight
read of one who died one morning,
                    but who also rose
to walk beneath the lintel, bearing petals in his palms.

The story is true.
A soul does not need to explain itself.
While the world turned toward light,
wind lifted the petals from his hands —
                a cloud of wings,
            a hundred sudden flames.

Soul

Across the chasm of flown things,
we arrived together, early in our future,
she a house of light, a lamp
which could not be dimmed.
                    Phosphorescent.
In childhood, she thought the trees
a ladder to heaven, and pushed us
                    higher, higher.

                    While I slept
she'd hear God walking above us.
          That's the furnace, I told her.
She pointed to the moon, lit and round —
                    surely it was home —
until I opened my school book
and pointed to the page.
                    She tried to dig her way back
with a spoon, made me hold out my palms
grimy with dirt,
                    studied them like a map.

There was the problem
                    of the lost father.
She could not give me his name or face.
And the men and boys who pinned me down.
And wars within the house,
                    and wars without.
Together we whispered of death
and how to achieve it.
                    By water, by blood.
One day she said to me
with the imperative of a parent,
          Write this. Write it down.
With her, this journey has been long.

Ending and Beginning

It is the heart's privilege
                    to love what it loves:
its own first abandonment,
the rose that gravity and rain
                    have overcome,
the shadowed space behind a door
where my mother, recently born
                    into her death, waits,
her tongue a tarnished spoon
                        filling with dust.

Between ending and beginning,
lonely from her dying,
                    my mother stitches a home
in the small eternity of night, in the time
when clocks wind down toward stillness,
                    before the birds
rise and scatter the seeds of morning.

And though death has sealed her mouth,
her face tells me that since the judgment,
her name is Sorrow,
                        her song, Lament;
                    Autumn, her regret.

It is the heart's privilege
to grieve what it grieves:
                    the leaves of the sky
what the trees have lost,
the ground's frost
                    what the sky has lost.
I tell my mother I lost her all my life,
and find her now, fugitive,
her life a dream, my childhood
                    swallowed in its throat,
the heart's privilege to shroud itself
in darkness, be chained to the past,
to stumble into the ragged dark,
                    each night open
to the thousand mouths of silence.

A stranger to the world, she refuses
to fold the linens in the drawer,
                    to count and recount
her necklace of pearls, reciting her prayers:
one, that her lover come
                    and rescue the day;
two, that the day take off his dark robes
and lie down to wine and ravishing.

But the time for prayer is over. My mother
turns, sudden, and leaves by no door,
        just as on the morning of her dying,
and with nothing in her arms.

Doorway

In a common doorway
        of a house I lived in,
the air between earth and heaven
                thinned.
Summer solstice, evening light
and the deer feeding in the quiet
field.
             The air said
I was to bring to you my pure soul.
My search was complete, said the air.

I gave account to heaven
        for the shoes worn through,
tears in my clothing, despair
over eternity's impossible logic
testing what we could do, suddenly
awakened on foreign soil, knowing
           we had lost everything.

And by increments must build it back.
Gathering the shattered pieces, stars
        strewn across the ground.
A God's-eye view.

And so I brought my soul
        to your soul, and the two
recognized each other.

        Soul said, be careful
what you tell to the others,
        still in mourning,
about the doorway —
appearing to be made of wood and air.
Better to say nothing at all.

The Dead

They go in the crystal hour, changed and human,
the hour before the horses wake
                              and move into the sun.
I carry them as I carry the sea in my hands,
the old ones hidden beneath the sky's dark wing.

— — —

When they took her to be burned,
evicted, she packed up her childhood,
the air between the kitchen dishes, her bitter cup.
She left without ears, without eyes or mouth,
                                        without feet.
She became a fish swimming through the waters,
became darkness, the moon fallen asleep
inside its own night, surrounding its own mourning.

— — —

I watch the scribbled stars change places,
        their cursive sentences vanish,
letters from the dead spreading the news.
This, a resting place only,
                              a cave, an inn, a hut.
Their peace our everlasting disquiet.

Death Unmoored Her

Death unmoored her,
     and we,
launching our little boats, our
torches lit,
rowed out some distance
     into the dark
in search of her.
But already she'd sailed ahead
where they waited, who knew everything
she had done
    and left undone.

And whispered among ourselves
of the way Death had come
traitorous into the room,
how she spurned his advances,
    the bouquets of roses,
as the sly knife sliced the rope.

We shored our boats and stood
on the great bluffs over the sea,
but could glimpse no trace of her —
     skeptic Thomas
sailing into the dawn and doubting
the forgiving masses
come to meet her, both
   the throngs rejoicing,
and the high-toned singing.

Three Coins

And my name is not my name.
And my dreams are the sleep of a stranger.

While my head was turned to watch
the stream of light a snail left in my path,
my mother turned to ash.
                Whole cities went with her,
countries whose names she swallowed,
my claim to this world.

Every day now the orphaned rain
searches for the river
         that is the house of her father.
I carried a torn dream through childhood.
                 I didn't know:
would my father wait for me before dying?

In my fist, three coins —
one to buy my passage from sorrow to wonder,
             one to purchase patience
from the clocks ticking their unhurried hours,
a third imprinted with the face
           of the one who must be found.

The mother who sewed her tongue to her mouth
and the mother whose ashes flew like moths
                              are the same mother.
And the child who sings to call back the forsaken
and the child whose ears ring with silence
                              are the same child.
And leaves which hold the rain
and leaves which spill moonlight
                              are the same leaves.

In earth the tree's roots tangle in sleep.
And though the child has become a woman
                  who lies with her lover,
she holds her childhood beneath her pillow
                              and wakens at night,
one hand on the rise and fall of its breath.

How Long

I listened for years, and one evening heard *home*
murmured among the grasses, the birds
knitting twigs and straw
                    into light and shadow,
the iris shedding her burial clothes.

How long must we wait
until the clocks chime resurrection,
till angelus bells echo the foxes' praise?

If my father were to answer, he'd point
to the decades he opened and shut
                    the stunned doors of houses
and wondered if his daughter, night's hostage,
would arrive to a vacant house.

I'd tell of the years the mirrors filled with snow,
when branches huddled under white cloth
                    signifying a death, the world,
the wrung muscle in my chest measuring
room after room,

until my father, holding my name in his mouth,
spoke a mystery beyond his own understanding,
carved a canyon the width of bereavement
over which the birds sailed, gleaning
            the sum of our loneliness.

Now his hands forge clay into bowls.
In one, he weighs his tears,
in another lie all his stories speaking at once.
In a third, he gathers up the names for redemption —
both the light burning and the lamp,
                    both feather and wind,
the ransomed hours pooled in our hands.

Remembered Future

The morning I slithered onto the bright
                    coin of the world,
my mother turned her head away.
Already, my father was lost.
Only the quick rush of blood
through my infant heart and out again
                    held me to this world.

From my earliest beginnings, I dreamt
                    my father's hands
that laid stone upon stone, that like him,
did their grieving in silence,
                    their faces wet all winter.

In my dream, my father built a road
so that the sea might find him.
He was a bird, though the work broke his wings.
I was a fish with torn fins
                    caught in a river of moonlight
until a song about our remembered future
rose from the sea, and my white throat.

Now, my desires are simple: to be a cricket
                    in my father's house, to live
among his books and papers and watch
his hands stitch one word to the next;
to sleep beneath his roof, hearing the stars
                    tell their stories to the sea.

Only the clouds silence the night.
And who wakes in us but God
                  and the astonished heart,
my father's hands two owls keeping watch
while he sleeps his holy sleep,
                  and coyotes call to the stars,
and summon the moon, the night's priest,
                        to raise her ivory host.

– III –

The Book of Astonishments

a book that opens onto night, the moon
a branch holding a fallen leaf and a ragged shirt
a buck, alert, vine tangled in his antlers

a child waiting through childhood for her father
a cluster of ferns the colour of cream

a flock of birds blown into the air
a horse nuzzling snow, last summer's grass
a mirror reflecting an empty room
a mirror reflecting billowed curtains
a motion in a window — a woman dancing

a paint jar spilled, paint on the kitchen floor and brushes,
                                        the canvas half white
a river, a wide valley, and wheat
a river of stone
a road which ends in sky

a wind lifting his silvered hair, and above, flocks of crows
a woodpecker tapping a rain-muffled tree
a wren's heart, discarded, and feathers

air alert, waiting in the cold for the bell to shatter it
all the colours from abandonment to tears
all the events of his life blown back to her
almost human, we disappeared into our skin

an eagle, bent over a fish in its claws
an owl feather on wet stone
and he bitten thin by weather, by waiting, the years
and time with needle and thread sews the leaves by latitudes,
                                        and the rain

annulet, anthem, antiphonal, aurora
answer them, answer with bread broken in both your hands
apples eaten to the core, still on the branch, flocks of thrushes
as ancient as the world itself

before the abandoned farmhouse, lilacs in bloom
begin again to gather the last hours of light

bells with their tongues pulled out, and only wind
                                        could sound them
beneath her longitudes, the sea remembers her lost ships

beseech, breath, bunch grass, burn
between layers of sleep when she knows why she is living
blue light beneath the snow more than cathedral windows

books scattered like leaves over the floor
broken with the past, as though nothing of the dead
                                        will come back

burned circles of slash now turned to ash and mud
by nightfall, the milky way spilled across the dark
by water, by blood, by memory, by forgetting

calyx, canticle, corona, crucible
candles climbing down from their perches, one wing
                                        attempting flight

candle whose flame becomes two in the window
clouds knotted in front of the moon
clouds that hold snow as if in a fist

crossing above the pines, a sea plane, the silence broken
crows alighting on the highest branches

curtains frayed with age blown into the room, over the bed,
and light shaken out across the floor
cut glass vase gathering dust in a vacant room

darkling, desolate, diminish, diurnum
darkness is not dark to you, the night is as bright as the day;
darkness and light to you are both alike
delicate, these tracks in snow, small as an infant's hands
discomfited, impatient, poised to flee but cannot
distant, the hills turn to indigo

do I dare praise the light, do I dare praise the world?

doors open at either end of the world, some entering,
others vanishing
doors open into vacant rooms, the house's blank stare
doors that open into nothing, doors that open into air

down, a brown bird's, strewn on the path
dried mud on the horses' faces, their flanks, their manes

each footstep vanishing in snow, the day drained of colour
each room holding a polished stillness, a fragile light
early light after a storm, the air a stained parchment

earthly, effulgent, evensong, eyrie

empty pages on which he recorded every detail
of his life on earth
eternity on either side: a window, a book, an owl, a leaf
even clouds leave their brief darkness on the earth

every window framed the sky
eyebrows on his weathered face whitened by snow

face in a window changed in wind, a different face in rain
fallen to the ground, the light between leaves
falling out of yesterday into open want

feral cats watching from the hay, a horse standing
                                        in the open door
fireweed where great trees have burned and wolves' eyes
                                        yellowed the night
flame, flute, fugue, full moon
fog rising on the mountain in the manner of smoke

gaze, ghost ship, graven, guardian spirit
god could find us if he wanted to, could unlock the hours
                                        holding us to earth

going down into the small rooms darkness knows
grief I will carry into the places of rain

hapax legomenon, hoarfrost, house finch, hyssop
has tragedy visited us? It would seem so
he carried petals, petals in his mouth you know
he lit candles and pressed them into the snow
he, missing for years as though he were an outline in chalk

hinges stiffened by rain, by wind, latch rusted on a barn door
his earliest questions blown back to him
his life began again, but death had changed him
his soul lingered in the room, watched us bend over him

hoofprints frozen into earth, a dozen dark moons
hoofprints in mud filled with urine and rain
horses standing in a field, one with its head over the other's back
horses with snow on their backs, manes tangled by wind

how bright in winter the ochre branches
how did I come to this life, searching for others once known
how quickly the moon waned, and the night
how to describe this world to those left behind

I can only tell you what happened, what I saw
I count new trunks sprouted from the stump
I do not know what shape these hours will take
I had hoped for some ecstatic utterance, no matter how ordinary

I have mothered two who arrived in my belly slippery as salmon
I have never left the place of my longing

iki, illuminate, incunabula, invocation
in another time, another place, they had been inseparable
indigo, roan, sorrel, dun — the horses' manes meet the grass

in his eyes, sight beyond blindness
in the end, it didn't matter what I believed

in the interval between my birth and my dying

in the moon's absence his hands felt to her like thick wings
in this bright hour, this unearthly stillness
in this far place, the world, salt in our hair, an east wind

into a light unexpected, both the living and the dead
island of shadow moving across a field

it was more than simple praise, the coyote, the dawn
it was simple, really — I was changed in an instant
its door is the rain, its window, evening

jacaranda, jack pine, japonica, jubilate
journey across borders, the black smoke of a train
journey of forty-one years; then, a house made of rain
journey requiring both body and soul
just now wakened, she crept downstairs where he had lit the stove,
   and she saw him, hands folded, in the first light of day

keep me as the apple of an eye; hide me under the shadow of your wings

kire, kudlik, kwakiutl, kyrie
knocking on the door of an empty house

knotted her hands that swept the floor, the yard,
    the earth hard and shining
knowing him by his voice before she saw his face

lacewing, lantern, leaf, legato
language torn from ancient tongues, carried on the sea,
      spilling onto stone
late afternoon and already the moon is lit
letters bundled in stained string

light, sorrow, souls in their cages of flesh
lilacs bloomed there, beside a gate, the field
    an imperceptible green
lined with dirt, his palms a map

listening, wondering if what is alive will remain alive
lit candles in the Mission San Xavier del Bac,
   and in the doorway a slant of light

magus, matins, mono no aware
map with no roads, only the curved lines of elevation,
     how close to the sky
maple seeds caught on barbed wire
mare in labour, not yet dawn, she played Mozart
    through a barn window

memory of the one she searched for all her life
moon half-obscured by rain
moon in the snow-lined branches, moon ringed with frost

moss grown along the trunks of trees
moss on the stone marking the horse's grave
mud on her pants, hay on her socks

music, sleeping in the piano, which she wakened with her fingers
my dead do not whisper in my ear, do not cry behind a door

my father walking alone in his mind
my father walking alone, the road a corridor of sky and pine
my father with bread broken in both his hands

my garments worn through, instruments of the wind
my hands folding past and future, memory and longing

nach und nach, narcissus, nebula, nunc dimittis

night in winter, full moon, cold and shadows
night making moons of the snow-white stones
night of absence, hour of waiting

no one can say it didn't happen
nor one, nor two, nor three in sacrifice can stop the world
                                                    from dying
not that the door closed, or that it was locked; the door is gone

nothing disturbed his slow breathing
nothing left on the tree but apples

obelisk, oblation, o magnum mysterium
on a cluttered desk, a letter which begins, "Dear Creator,"
on the writing table a piece of white paper, a pen
one eye saw only shadow, the other took in everything

one raven rowing through the sky on its black oars
one thing he said: *everything begins and ends in stillness*
only light lies down where her bed had been

or a leaf impaled on barbed wire
or fire, star-fed behind the owl's perch
or the frozen grasses bending near the gate
or your face in that moment, utterly alive before your death

overnight, frost has settled on the leaves
owls mating in the night, the cedar holding them in one hand

palimpsest, pavane, primordial, psalter
palms outstretched toward rain and grief
past, what once was present, we carry in our faces
perplexed with this life, it goes on and goes on

photographed from above, the farmhouse when it was alive,
                                        the fields, and summer
pile of manure on the path; someone come to greet the horses
ploughed under, the house now a field of wheat,
                              the air's rasped whisper
poured into the horses' trough at morning — sunlit water

present becoming past, past opening all its doors to the present

quail, quake, quantum, quetzal
quickly he wrote in traditional script, his hand
                              crossing the page, a memory
quiet predations of wolves, twilit, a field fence, and snow
quiet, the path before it becomes the meadow

quotidian, the dawn, his clothes folded carefully over the chair,
                                        his watch stopped at 3:12

radiant, remnant, requiem, root
rain like small birds perched on fence wire
rain marking her face
rain-streaked, the window, and he by firelight reading from a book

rivers of salmon: Okanagan, Pasayten, Similkameen, Tulameen
road leading to the horizon between endless green wheat
rusted fence post, grief, letters scratched on leaves to those
                                        missing from the world

sabi, sanctus, sonata, stone
say, *flame,* say *swan, the spread of their wings at the torn edge of dawn*
she kept these lines hidden, slipped into the pillowcase on her
        bed beside a window, and below, winter-blooming jasmine
she remembers the house of her childhood, floor of polished
                                        earth and also the yard
she ties knots in her breath where they lie examining the stars
she will say it too late, the wind having blown the door
                                        open, then shut

silence interrupted by birds
silence, the wasp nest in winter
slender alder a lantern among the pines
slip of paper read *return,* the handwriting unrecognized
smoke from a chimney rising among the pines

snow falling against your face, the moonless light
snow that rose to cover the windows, the rooms cast in darkness
so that someone coming after would know how it was
                                        in those days, how we loved

solitary in his cloister, the moose prays for grass;
                       I ask for dust, bindweed only
some nights I hear them in their dark basements, these hearts
some part of his soul lived inside her, even before she knew him

sometimes the eyes do not tell the truth
sound like a held breath escaping
sputter of her lungs as she slept, her breath in the room
                           and frost growing on the walls

stars spilling their light like leaves in rain
stuttering fires that were burning inside him

such waiting, for snow to fill the fir, for the moon to make
                               its nest of light
sudden buds on the willow, its sap running gold

talon, tamarack, tenebrae, tongue
teacup and chipped saucer, oil cloth spread over a table,
                                 breadcrumbs
the ancient scent of a childhood not her own

the heart's pendulum, he told her, and she remembered, even
                              as an old woman
the path paved with wet leaves
the river jammed with ice like shattered glass
the scent of cedar in the heat

the train carried mountains in its windows
the trellis overcome with roses
the troubled hours, a psalm, a prayer
the *Tsilhqut'in,* looking west, pointed with their chins

the water trough lined with silt
the world a place where all worlds collide

their beaks and claws, the knuckles of their feet, small
                                    packages of grief

there are centuries whose happiness we have forgotten
there are no words for this
these are the only words I have with which to tell you
these words are holy: *ember, birdsong, exile, plum, witness, kiss*

this is what I saw: all light ancient, all darkness
thoughtless, the flowers in this field come back, and back
three flames of a candle reflected in a window

to name the hours, to see the world as it is and decide to live
to repair his sight by some act of contrition
to sew an aster into the chest of a drowned man

toward *the mountains that bleed,* the path to the sea.
two boulders covered in moss, then leaves

umber, unbending, unction, utter
under an umbrella watching him disappear down a road,
                                    his life trailing behind him
under the moon, horses wade to their shoulders in pine-shadow

unforeseen, her hand over his mouth, her hand over her own
unspoken, the soul searches for one last known
                                    in the other world
unspoken water, stone, a ring of light, eyes of owls
                                    and behind them, stars

vanishing, each second, each minute, each hour, each day,
                                    each year
vanishing, the darkness at dawn
vanishing, the end point of light

verdigris, vestige, vigil, visitant
vespers, a fox shadowed in low sun, then nothing
                              on the flat horizon

viola with broken strings, tendril shoots from wood
violin with the scent of resin and memory

visible, earth in the creases of his face
voice that came from no mouth but the night

wabi, warbler, whalebone, winter
walking in snow and moonlight and the pines' dark water
waves, the sea's long manes, the shore

we begin, slowly at first, to remember
what I have left undone
what keeps us here — swift rush of blood through the heart

what name will I answer to?
when and whom have I failed to love

when rain marked her face
when sleep took him, when death in its wooden boat

when sparrows rose at once and the air filled with rain and wings
when the words strike, you will rise and will not know yourself

when you are finished with this life

where does the story end and begin
where his footprints did not mold the earth, where
                              he did not keep a house
while reading the poems of a great poet still unknown
                              in many parts of the world

who sent me into this life and for what purpose
whose voice, behind my head in the dark

wind escaping the boundaries of silence
wire-thin branch bent over a fence
with water from an ivory jar she knelt and washed
                                    his head, then his feet

woodpecker again; still can't see him
words rose from his mouth and flew like birds into air

words rose inside him and became a river, became
                    the stillness of night, his life a holy book
would I make this journey again, another life

x the imaginary middle of the ring where she halted the horse
                                    and the horse bowed its head

xalam, xanadu, xat, xebec

yangtze, yellow-headed blackbird, yew, yggdrasil
yearning, a litany of absence, and light fallen
                                    onto her open palms

years of light and dust collected in one barn
yellow, the colour of pine dust and bone, a cedar gate
                                    on which blackbirds stood
you stood alone on the porch, smoke of your cigarette
                                    rising, a soul

you told me, *write this — write it down*
you were looking out your window that moment
                                    and saw it happen

you with your smoke-coloured hair, the stubble on your chin
your hair silvered by the time I arrived

zeitgeist, time's ghost, is born then flies from the earth,
                            and another arrives, and another
zenith, zia, zocalo, zuni
zero hour, hour of matins, the bell tensed
                    in the moment before singing

Patrick Lane has called Pamela Porter "a poet to be grateful for." Her poems have earned numerous accolades, including the inaugural Gwendolyn MacEwan Poetry Prize, the 2013 *Malahat Review* 50th Anniversary Poetry Prize, the *Our Times* Poetry Award for political poetry, the 2012 *FreeFall* Magazine Poetry Award, the 2011 *Prism International* Grand Prize in Poetry, and the 2010 *Vallum* Magazine Poem of the Year Award. She was also a finalist for the Raymond Souster, the Pat Lowther and the CBC poetry prizes. Her novel in verse, *The Crazy Man*, won the 2005 Governor General's Award, the Canadian Library Association Book of the Year for Children Award, the TD Canadian Children's Literature Award, and other prizes. Pamela lives near Sidney, B.C., with her family and a menagerie of rescued horses, dogs, and cats.